Betcha Didn't Know!

BLACK WOMEN IN HISTORY CRAFT AND ACTIVITY BOOK

CREATED BY AMARI ROBINSON

Copyright © 2023 by Amari Robinson.

All rights reserved.
No portion of this book may be reproduced in any form without written permission from the publisher or authors, except as permitted by U.S. copyright law. For permission requests, contact WEBDMG at info@webdmg.com.

Acknowledgements...

Thanks to my Mommy and Daddy for the tools they have given me to do this book and their amazing support. Thank you for my siblings for doing some the crafts with me! I love you all so much! And thank you to Mr. Cameron, CamDaIllaStrata, for the awesome illustrations!

Betcha Didn't Know!

BLACK WOMEN IN HISTORY
CRAFT AND ACTIVITY BOOK

TABLE OF CONTENTS

- 2   JACKIE ORMES
- 6   SHERYL SWOOPES
- 9   HATTIE MCDANIEL
- 13   FRANCES ELLEN WATKINS HARPER
- 16   DR. MARIE CLARK TAYLOR
- 20   DIANNE DURHAM
- 23   GWENDOLYN BROOKS
- 27   KATHERINE JOHNSON
- 32   ZELDA BARBOUR WYNNE-VALDES
- 36   JUNE BACON-BERCEY
- 39   BRIANNA SCURRY
- 42   MAYME AGNEW CLAYTON
- 45   DR. GLADYS WEST
- 50   MAGGIE LENA WALKER
- 53   DR. JANET BASHEN
- 57   WILMA RUDOLPH
- 60   DR. MARIAN CROAK
- 64   DR. MARIE M. DALY
- 68   ABOUT THE AUTHOR

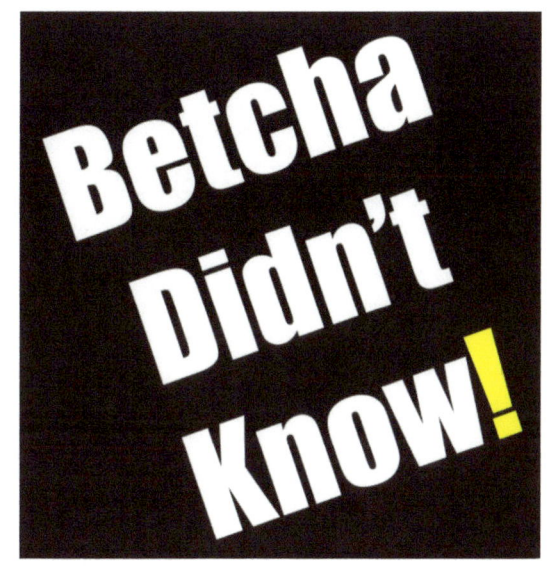

Hey y'all! I Betcha Didn't Know about...this book!!! I am Amari Robinson and this is the Betcha Didn't Know! Black Women in History Craft and Activity Book where I tell you a little bit about 18 important African American women that I think are amazing! I am homeschooled and for many years, I have researched African American women. I have been amazed over and over by what I have learned and I think you should know about these extraordinary people too!

With this book, you will learn about these amazing women, color their pictures and complete a craft or activity associated with them! I have also included the podcast episodes were I talk all about each of these women so you can also listen to my podcast while doing the craft or activity!

I hope y'all enjoy this book! And remember, you are dope know it and show it! Bye everyone!

-Amari Robinson

I betcha didn't know about
Jackie Ormes

Ms. Jackie Ormes was the first African-American woman to be a cartoonist!

Jackie Ormes

LISTEN TO THE EPISODE!

Jackie Ormes

Create a Jackie Ormes Charicature!

Materials: Copy of the shapes on the next page, crayons or coloring pencils, craft stick, scissors, glue

1. First make a copy of the shapes on the next page. Color them the indicated colors.
2. Cut out all the shapes.
3. Take the big brown circle and the black hair and glue it partly on the brown circle.
4. Next, glue the white circles and black circles to make eyes and put them on the big circle below the hair.
5. Then, take the little brown circles and glue them behind the big brown circle. These are her ears.
6. Put the red lips on at the bottom.
7. Grab a black marker and draw her a little crescent shaped nose.
8. Lastly, glue the stick on the back and you're done! 😃

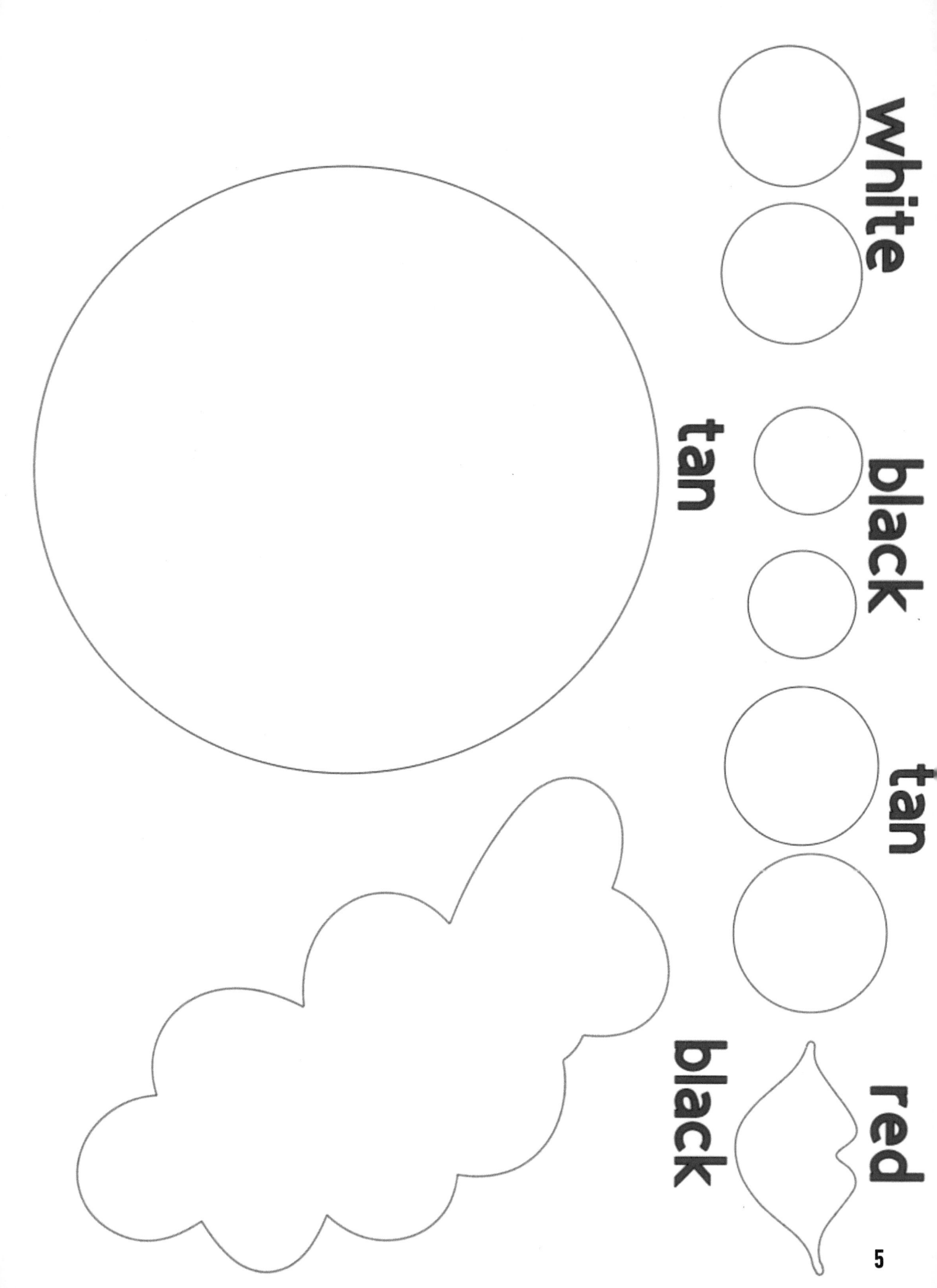

I betcha didn't know about
Sheryl Swoopes

Ms. Sheryl Swoopes was a professional basketball player and she was the first player to be signed to the WNBA!

Sheryl Swoopes

LISTEN TO THE EPISODE!

Sheryl Swoopes

Ms. Sheryl was an AMAZING basketball player! Get outside and practice your dribbling skills!

When practicing your drilling skills, be sure to:

- Use your fingertips to dribble- it allows you to control the ball more easily.
- Only dribble with one hand! (Using two hands is an illegal action called double dribble.)
- Keep the ball as low as possible. The ball should bounce between your knees and hips, but it should never go above the hips.
- Keep your head up - this allows you to tell where the ball is without looking at it.

I betcha didn't know about
Hattie McDaniel

Ms. Hattie McDaniel was the first African American woman to win an Oscar!

Hattie McDaniel

LISTEN TO THE EPISODE!

Hattie McDaniel

Ms. Hattie won an Oscar for her work in a movie. Create your own award for your hard work or give it to someone that deserves it!!

Materials: cardstock paper (your color of choice), ruler, scissors, glue

1. Get card stock in any color you want or you can do different colors for different parts.
2. You need to cut out two 11" x 2" strips, then cut out two 4" x 1.5" strips.' Now find a circle to trace with that is about 2.5" across.
3. After you find the circle, trace it and cut out.
4. Now with grab the short rectangles and cut triangles on the end of them.
5. With the big rectangles from the end measure 1/2" draw a line or a dot so you know where to fold.

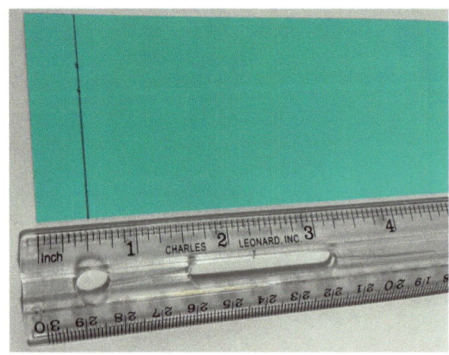

Hattie McDaniel

5. Now turn the whole thing over where the fold is facing the table, the next piece line it up with the other fold. Do that all the way down, and on the other piece of paper, too.

6. Attach it like this with hot glue.

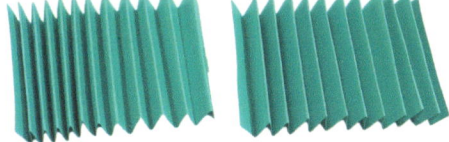

7. And now on the other side with hot glue.

8. Now push it down  with one hand and the other hand put hot glue on The circle and put it on the on the folded paper then turn it over and press on it to get it to stick.

9. Before you do the other side, write something encouraging on the circle. Then hot glue it to the folded paper circle.

10. Now add the small rectangles to the bottom like a ribbon. All done!

I betcha didn't know about
Frances Ellen Watkins Harper

Ms. Frances Ellen Watkins Harper was the first African American woman to publish a short story and co-founded a major organization for women of color!

Frances Ellen Watkins Harper

LISTEN TO THE EPISODE!

Frances Ellen Watkins Harper

WORD SEARCH

```
W P O E T O W S U C X L I J T E D A
O N R Z G W N I F R A N C E S S X N
Q Z L C J L I T E R A T U R E H J T
S E A M S T R E S S I K W B Q O E I
W R K Y H N C B I M Y M D X N R L S
W N Y J N X B V P X G U D H T T B L
O B F O R E S T L E A V E S U S H A
M V A B O L I T I O N I S T L T W V
E Q U A L I T Y O B F C G U L O J E
N J M H T G A U T H O R X R K R H R
E X J E D U C A T I O N E L B Y J Y
F A U N V I W U U N N T J O J S M E
```

Find the following words in the puzzle.
Words are hidden → ↓ and ↘

ABOLITIONIST
ANTISLAVERY
AUTHOR
EDUCATION
EQUALITY

FORESTLEAVES
FRANCES
LITERATURE
POET
SEAMSTRESS

SHORTSTORY
WOMEN

I betcha didn't know about
Dr. Marie Clark Taylor

Dr. Marie Clark Taylor was the first African-American woman to earn a PhD in botany!

Dr. Marie Clark Taylor

LISTEN TO THE EPISODE!

Dr. Marie Clark Taylor

Dr. Marie was a botanist! Make a beautiful flower using some recycled materials!

Materials: 4 sheets of tissue paper, ruler, scissors, 4 chenille sticks, empty water bottle or class bottle

1. Take 4 sheets of tissue paper and place them one above the other. Measure 4 inches and fold the tissue paper at that line. Grab your scissors and cut the paper on that line.
2. Fold the tissue papers in front- back pattern all the way to the end. Now it should look like rectangles on top of each other! Tie a chenille stick/pipe cleaner in the center of the tissue paper and twist it all the way down.
3. Slowly separate all the layers of tissue paper, to make the flower look like it has bloomed. On the last 2 layers, the layer that's on top goes up and the one on the bottom goes down.

Dr. Marie Clark Taylor

Dr. Marie was a botanist! Make a beautiful flower using some recycled materials!

Materials: 4 sheets of tissue paper, ruler, scissors, 4 chenille sticks, empty water bottle or class bottle

4. Turn the flower upside down and the tissue paper that is facing you put down with the other fluffed tissue paper. Then cup it in your hand and give it a squeeze.
5. Do those steps again until you have four. If you don't want to make the other flowers you stop here and go to the last step.
6. After you make all 4 twist all of the chenille sticks together to make one big flower, and fluff out the flower so it can look more full.
7. Now get a empty water bottle or a glass and use it as your vase!

Enjoy your beautiful flower in your favorite place of your house!

I betcha didn't know about
Dianne Durham

Ms. Dianne Durham was the first African American gymnast to win the all around women's US National Championship!

Dianne Durham

LISTEN TO THE EPISODE!

Dianne Durham

Ms. Dianne Durham was the first African American gymnast to win the all around in women's US National Championship! Show off your gymnastics skills by practicing your cartwheels!

1. Face front and put your good leg (the leg you kick hardest with) in the front. Stretch your arms and put your arms by your ears.
2. Lower your arms towards the ground while raising your back leg. Keep your arms straight by your ears.
3. Put your hands on the ground and turn your body sideways.
4. Push off your front leg and bring your back leg up into a 'V' position.
5. Lower your good leg as you lift the first hand off the ground.
6. Bring your other leg off the mat as you raise your other hand off the floor.
7. End in a lunge facing the opposite position of how you started.
8. Now keep practicing until you've got it . 😊

I betcha didn't know about
Gwendolyn Brooks

Ms. Gwendolyn Brooks is the first African American to receive a Pulitzer Prize!

Gwendolyn Brooks

LISTEN TO THE EPISODE!

Gwendolyn Brooks

Ms. Gwendolyn Brooks is the first African American to receive a Pulitzer Prize for her collection of narrative poetry! Rap music has fantastic examples of narrative poetry! Read this "narrative poem" by Dj Jazzy Jeff and The Fresh Prince. Then, work on writing your own narrative poem!

"The Fresh Prince of Bel-Air"

Now, this is a story all about how
My life got flipped-turned upside down
And I'd like to take a minute
Just sit right there
I'll tell you how I became the prince
of a town called Bel-Air

In West Philadelphia born and raised
On the playground was where I spent most of my days
Chillin' out, maxin', relaxin', all cool
And all shootin' some b-ball outside of the school

Gwendolyn Brooks

When a couple of guys who were up to no good
Started making trouble in my neighborhood
I got in one little fight and my mom got scared
She said, "You're movin' with your auntie and uncle in Bel-Air"

I whistled for a cab and when it came near
The license plate said, "Fresh" and it had dice in the mirror
If anything I could say that this cab was rare
But I thought "Nah, forget it, yo, holmes to Bel Air"

I pulled up to the house about seven or eight
And I yelled to the cabbie, "Yo holmes, smell ya later"
I looked at my kingdom
I was finally there
To sit on my throne as the prince of Bel-Air

Writers: Willard C. Smith / Jeffrey Townes
The Fresh Prince of Bel-Air lyrics ©

I betcha didn't know about
Katherine Johnson

Ms. Katherine Johnson was a brilliant mathematician. She did the math to launch many of NASAs most famous missions!

Katherine Johnson

LISTEN TO THE EPISODE!

Katherine Johnson

Create a Rocket!

Materials: toilet paper roll, construction paper (white or blue) cardstock paper, ruler, scissors, glue

1. Make a copy of page 23 with card stock paper
2. After you make a copy, color the shapes in the color(s) you want.
3. Then cut out the shapes, take a piece of light blue or white construction paper, measure around the paper roll on the construction paper. Cut it out, then glue one end of the paper on the roll. Roll the paper on the paper roll so it covers the whole thing then glue the lip of the paper on the paper that you rolled.
4. Now with the hexagons put the small ones on top of the big ones and glue them.
5. Get the flames and put them on top of each other, the big one first, then the medium one, last, but not least, the small on top.
6. Now with the cone fold it so it shapes a cone then glue it, and now wait for it to dry (about an hour).

Katherine Johnson

Create a Rocket!

Materials: toilet paper roll, construction paper (white or blue)cardstock paper, ruler, scissors, glue

7. Once everything is dry, get the stand and put in the roll. You can glue it or tape it. Then get the flames and put it in front of the stand. Glue or tape that also.

8. Now get the hexagons put one on the bottom of the roll and put then other one above. Now glue the top of the roll and put the cone on it it might come off so just let sit there until the glue dries and it will stay and you are done! 😊

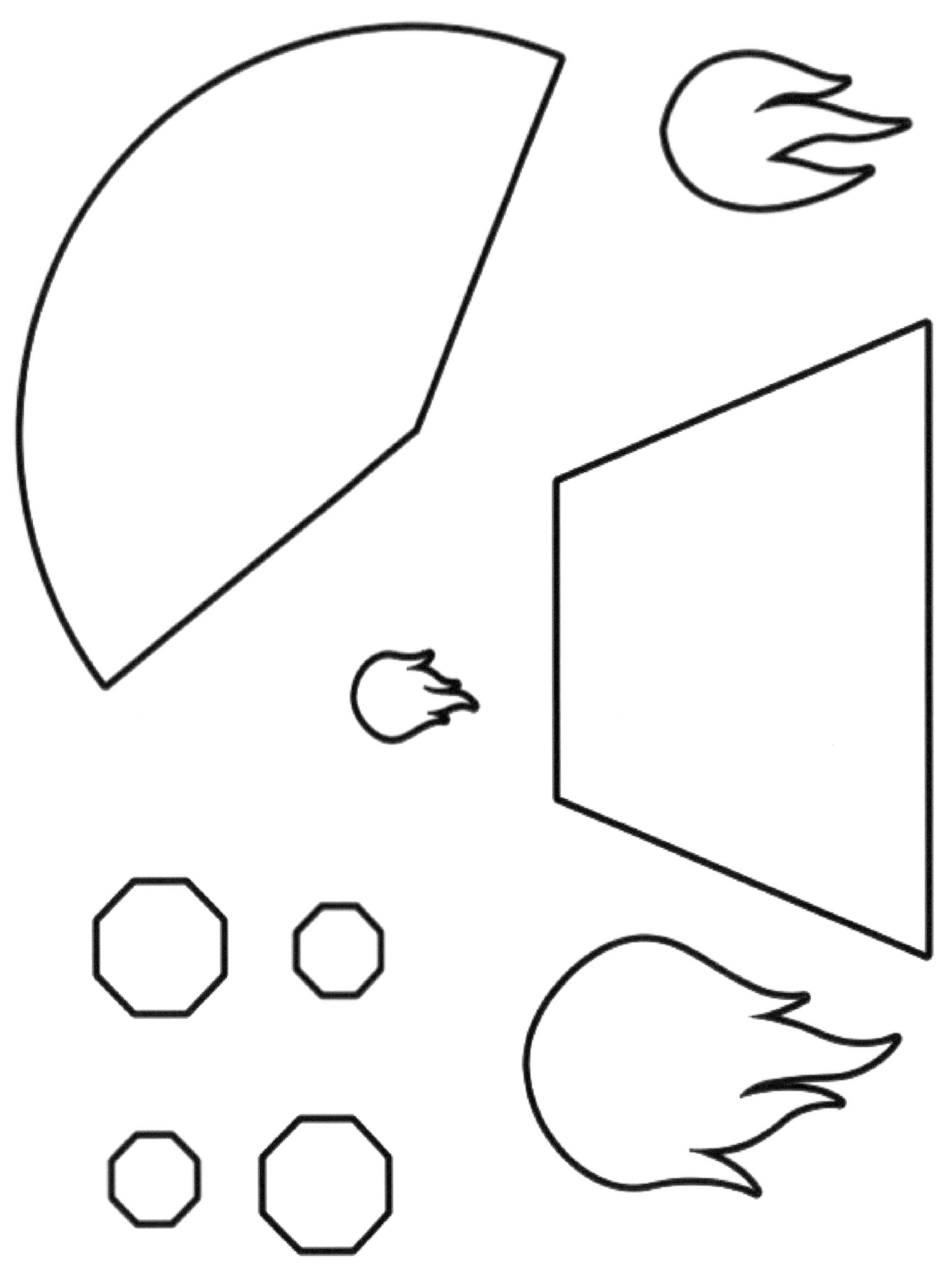

I betcha didn't know about
Zelda Barbour Wynn-Valdes

Ms. Zelda Barbour Wynn Valdes was an African American fashion and costume designer and the first black-owned business owner on Broadway in New York City!

Zelda Barbour Wynn-Valdes

LISTEN TO THE EPISODE!

Zelda Barbour Wynn-Valdes

Croquet Paper Dolls

Become a designer like Ms. Zelda!

Materials: cardstock paper, scissors, crayons, colored pencils or markers

1. Make a copy of the next page with card stock paper
2. Color the dolls and each of the pieces of clothing.
3. Cut out the dolls and clothing pieces.
4. Now, have fun making the boy handsome and the girl beautiful! Mix and match the pieces of clothing to see how many different outfits you can create!
5. Have fun! 😊

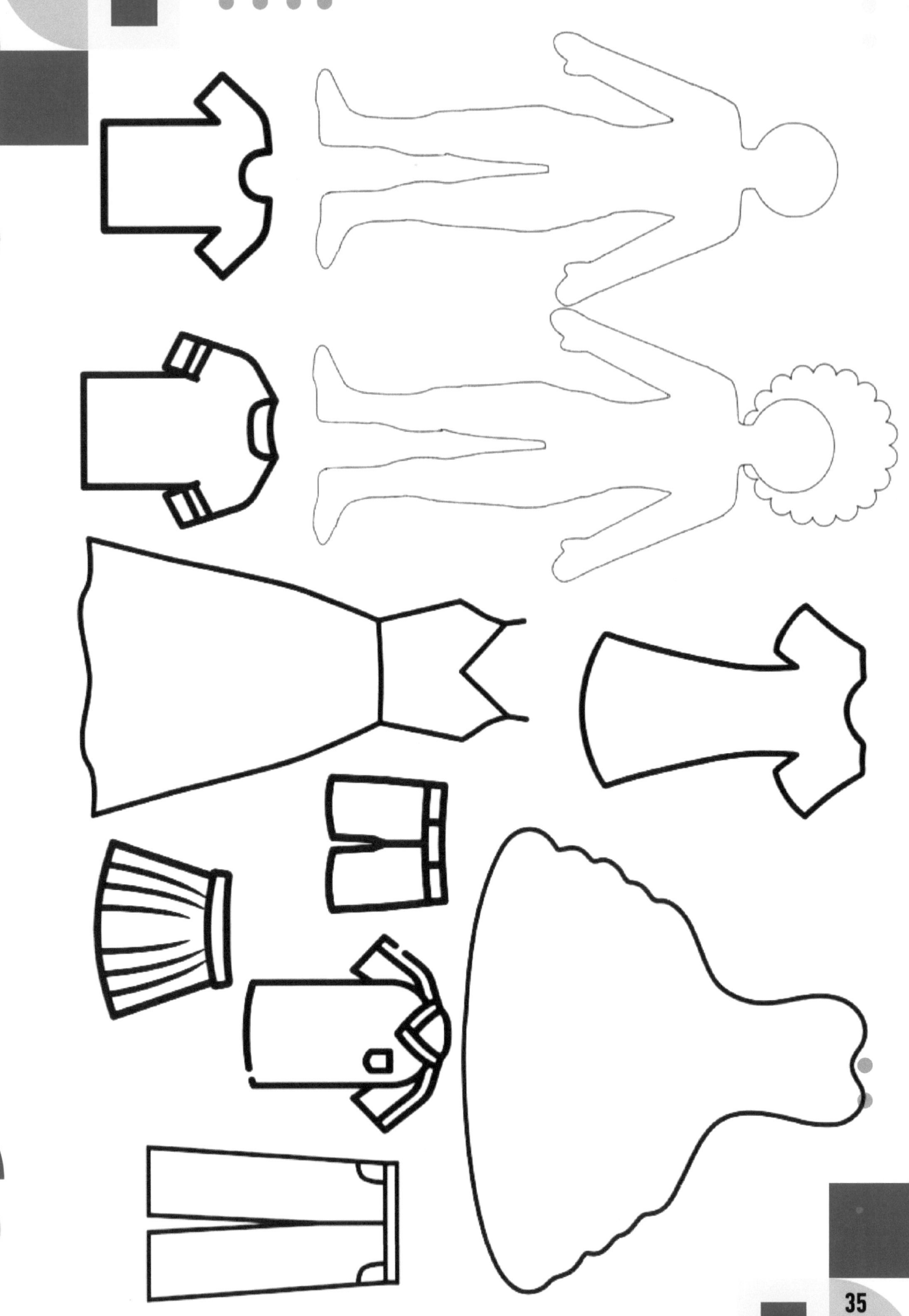

I betcha didn't know about
June Bacon-Bercey

Ms. June Bacon-Bercey was the first on-air African American female meteorologist!

June Bacon-Bercey

LISTEN TO THE EPISODE!

June Bacon-Bercey

Ms. June was a meteorologist. Observe your weather for a week and see if you are able to see any patterns. Is it cloudy, raining, sunny, partly cloudy, thunderstorming, snowing? What's the temperature?

	High/Low Temperature	Weather Conditions
Day 1		
Day 2		
Day 3		
Day 4		
Day 5		
Day 6		
Day 7		

I betcha didn't know about
Briana Scurry

Ms. Briana Scurry was an amazing soccer goalkeeper for the United States Women's national soccer team!

Briana Scurry

LISTEN TO THE EPISODE!

Briana Scurry

Ms. Briana was an amazing soccer player! Practice your soccer skills by learning to do tick tocks!

1. Start with the ball between your feet.
2. Slightly bend your knees.
3. Hit the ball with the inside of your feet like you are passing to yourself.
4. Then do that back and forth in between your feet.

Practice a few times and when you've got it, see how fast you can get to twenty tick tocks! Record your results below.

Trials	Time
Trial 1	
Trial 2	
Trial 3	

I betcha didn't know about
Mayme Agnew Clayton

Ms. Mayme Agnew Clayton was a librarian, and the founder and president of the largest privately held collection of African-American historical materials in the world!

Mayme Agnew Clayton

LISTEN TO THE EPISODE!

Mayme Agnew Clayton

Ms. Mayme was a collector of African American history! Take some time and make a collection of your own!

Below, catalog items that mean a lot to you! Write down the name of the item, where you found it, and, if you can, when it was created. Here are some examples of items you might want to seek out:

a special picture you drew
a souvenir from a trip
a project you created
your favorite book
a history book that you really like

Item Name	Where did you found it?	When was it created?

I betcha didn't know about
Dr. Gladys West

Dr. Gladys West's computer programming led to the creation of the Global Positioning System, GPS!

Dr. Gladys West

LISTEN TO THE EPISODE!

Dr. Gladys West

Dr. Gladys's programming uses satellites as a key part of our ability to use GPS. Create your own satellite!

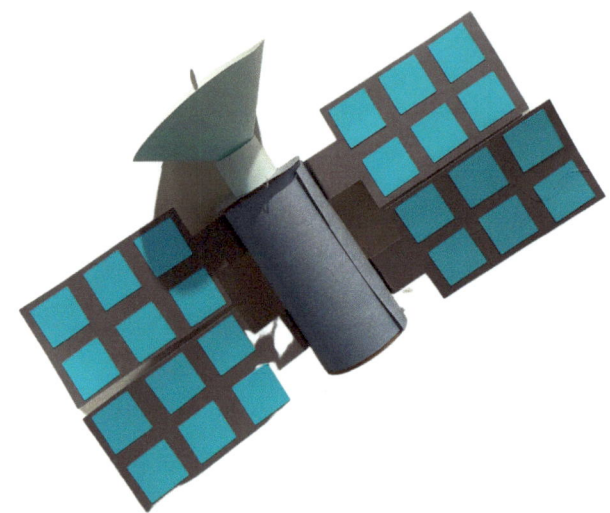

Materials: cardstock paper, construction paper (white or blue), toilet paper roll, scissors, crayons, colored pencils or markers

1. Make a copy of page 36 with cardstock paper.
2. After you make a copy, color the shapes in the colors you want.
3. Cut out the shapes, take a piece of light blue or white construction paper, measure around the paper roll on the construction paper. cut it out, then glue one end of the paper on the roll. Roll the paper on the paper roll so it cover the whole thing then glue the lip of the paper on the paper that you rolled. Now cut the squares and the 4 panels. Each panel gets six squares. Glue or hot glue them.
4. Grab the paper roll. With the same construction paper color, trace the top of the roll and cut the construction paper.

Dr. Gladys West

Dr. Gladys's programming uses satellites as a key part of our ability to use GPS. Create your own satellite!

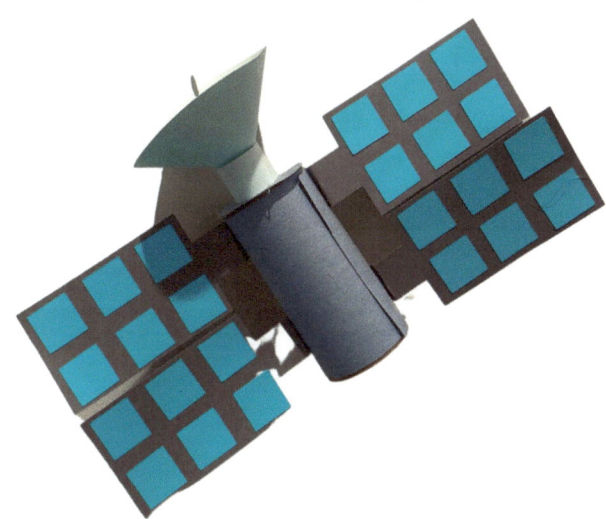

Materials: cardstock paper, construction paper (white or blue), toilet paper roll, scissors, crayons, colored pencils or markers

6. Cut out the cone (looks like PacMan), the rectangle strip, and the antenna (long rectangle with circle on top).
7. Fold the paper into a cone and glue it or tape it.
8. Get the rectangle strip and roll it and glue the lip of it, and glue the roll on the circle you cut out earlier.
9. Put the cone in the neck (the rectangle roll) and hot glue it on there. Now take the antenna and hot glue it in the cone.
10. Two panels go on each side of the paper roll. Hot glue them to the top of the satellite it might be hard, so ask a grownup to help you! All done!! 😊

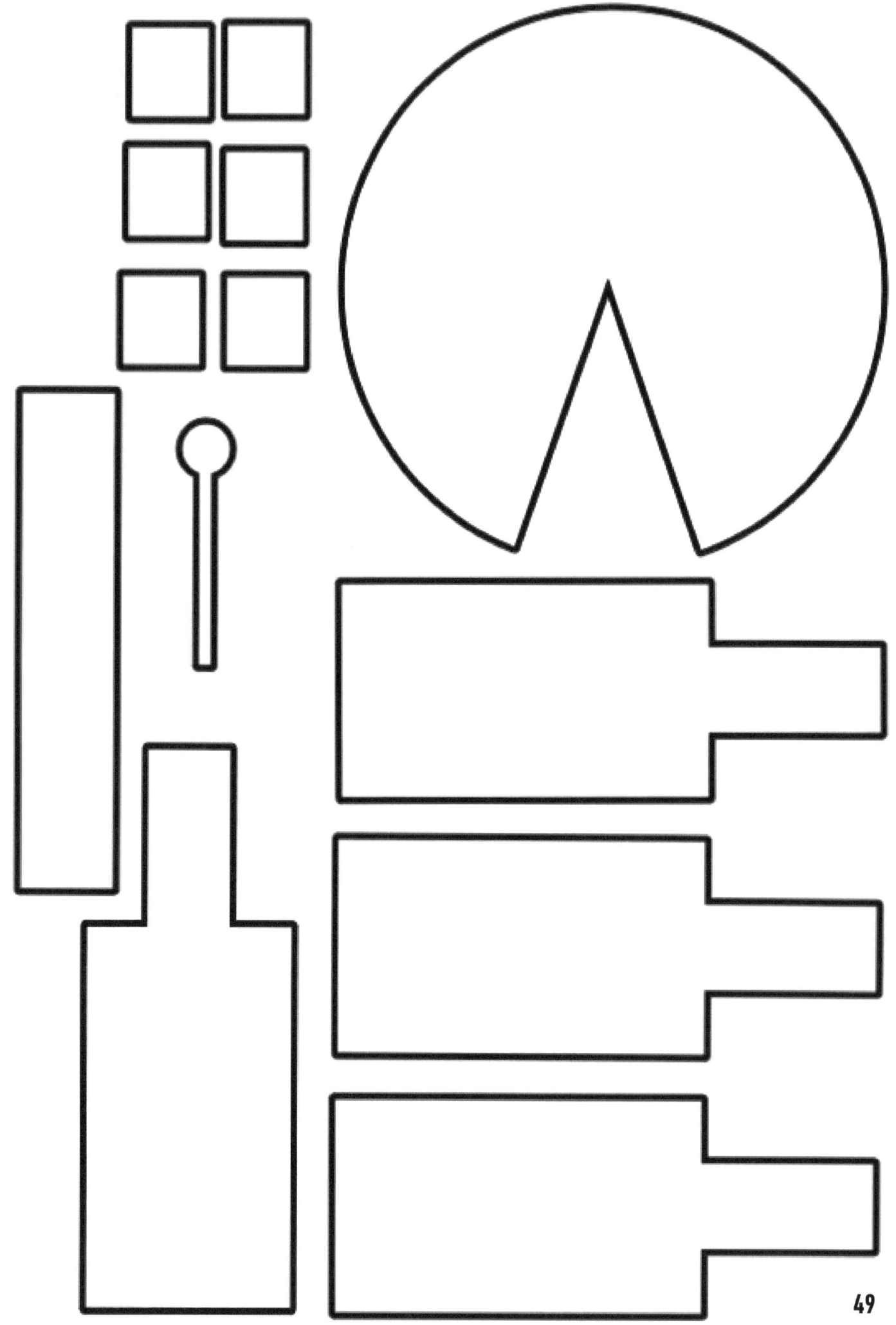

I betcha didn't know about
Maggie Lena Walker

Ms. Maggie Lena Walker was the first African American and first woman in the United States to found a bank!

Maggie Lena Walker

LISTEN TO THE EPISODE!

Maggie Lena Walker

Ms. Maggie was the first African American woman in the United States to found a bank! Make your own piggy bank using recycled materials!

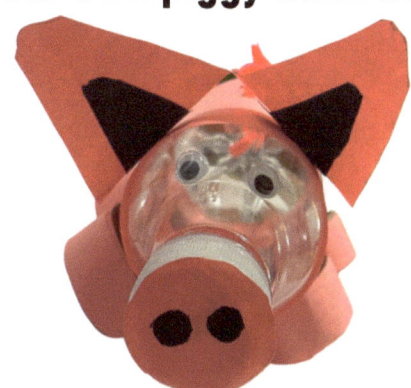

Materials: pink construction paper, used water bottle, 2 toilet paper rolls, crayons, black marker, googly eyes, tape, parent assistance hot glue with sharp scissors or knife

1. Get a used plastic water bottle.
2. Get pink paper and measure around the bottle. Cut it out and wrap it around the bottle. That is the stomach.
3. With the same pink paper trace the cap on the paper and cut it out. Draw two black circles on it. Tape or glue it to the top. That is the snout.
4. Cut out triangles using the pink and black paper. Big ones on pink, and small ones on black.
5. Fold the ears a little bit and hot glue it on the bottle. Then put googly eyes on the bottle and glue it.
6. Cut the paper rolls in half. Measure the roll on pink paper and wrap each piece around the roll and glue it. These will be the hooves.
7. Now hot glue the hooves on the pink covered water bottle.
8. Now, have an adult cut a rectangle on top big enough to fit a coin.

Now you're done! Enjoy! 😊

I betcha didn't know about
Dr. Janet Bashen

Dr. Janet Emerson Bashen is the first African American female to hold a patent for a software invention!

Dr. Janet Bashen

LISTEN TO THE EPISODE!

Dr. Janet Bashen

Dr. Janet is the first African American female to hold a patent for a software invention which is a BIG DEAL!! Use the magazine cover on the next page to create a magazine cover for Dr. Janet or something fantastic that you have done! Use the space below to write your rough draft.

WRITE HER/YOUR NAME AND A SHORT SENTENCE OF WHY SHE/YOU IS/ARE AMAZING!

_____

_____

_____

_____

WRITE AN INTERESTING STORY TITLE THAT MIGHT ALSO BE INCLUDING IN THIS MAGAZINE

_____

_____

VOL 29

INSPIRATION

MAGAZINE

DRAW DR. BASHEN'S PHOTO HERE

Person of the Year

WRITE HER NAME AND A SHORT SENTENCE OF WHY SHE IS AMAZING!

ADD AN INTERESTING STORY TITLE HERE

How Betcha Didn't Know! (BDK!) Podcast is Educating the world about African American Women

PERSON OF THE YEAR EDITION

I betcha didn't know about
Wilma Rudolph

Ms. Wilma Rudolph is the first American woman to win three gold medals in track and field at a single Olympics!

Wilma Rudolph

LISTEN TO THE EPISODE!

Wilma Rudolph

Ms. Wilma is an amazing track star.
Time to get outside and see how fast you can run!

1. Set your 'track' by marking the beginning and end of where you will run.
2. Get a timer (you can use your watch, phone, or have someone count for you).
3. Run as fast as you can!
4. See what your time is and write down. Do it again to see if you can improve it!

Trials	Time
Trial 1	
Trial 2	
Trial 3	

I betcha didn't know about
Dr. Marian Croak

Dr. Marian Croak was part of a team that made Voice over IP and was one of two first African American women to be inducted into the Women in Tech Hall of Fame!

Dr. Marian Croak

LISTEN TO THE EPISODE!

Dr. Marian Croak

Dr. Marian Croak was part of a team that made Voice over IP which is the tech behind FaceTime! Create your own Facetime phone!

Materials: 2 sheets construction or cardstock paper (any color), 1 sheet of white cardstock, ruler, scissors, glue

1. Chose the color of paper you want and cut out two 8x16cm rectangles. Round the corners with scissors.
2. With the another piece of paper (it can be the same or a different color), cut two 2x6cm and two 2x14cm rectangles. Take them and fold one side half way of the rectangle and fold the other side they both should meet in the middle.
3. Do that on all of the other rectangles. When you lift the flaps it should have 3 sides on all of them. Take one of the phone shapes and glue the short rectangles at the top and bottom of the phone. Now take the long rectangles and glue them on the side.

Dr. Marian Croak

Dr. Marian Croak was part of a team that made Voice over IP which is the tech behind FaceTime! Create your own Facetime phone!

Materials: 2 sheets construction or cardstock paper, ruler, scissors, glue

4. Take the other phone shape and hot glue it on the rectangles. Now get white card stock and cut out the same shape as the phone but a bit smaller so the color of the phone paper is showing a little bit on the sides.
5. Now draw a FaceTime call on the white paper. It can be you taking to your friend or someone in your family.
6. After you have drawn the FaceTime pictures, glue it or hot glue it on the phone.

You're done! Now you can make another and "FaceTime" another friend! 😊

I betcha didn't know about
Dr. Marie M. Daly

Dr. Marie M. Daly was the first Black American woman in the United States to earn a Ph.D. in Chemistry!

Dr. Marie M. Daly

LISTEN TO THE EPISODE!

Dr. Marie M. Daly

Dr. Marie's work would become important to heart health! The human heart is made of blood vessels which are hollow tubes that carry blood all over the body. The human body has three kind of vessels, arteries, veins and capillaries. Arteries carry blood away from the heart and veins carry blood toward the heart. Capillaries are very small blood vessels that connect arteries to the veins.

ARTERIES
Color number 1 areas red

VEINS
Color number 2 areas blue

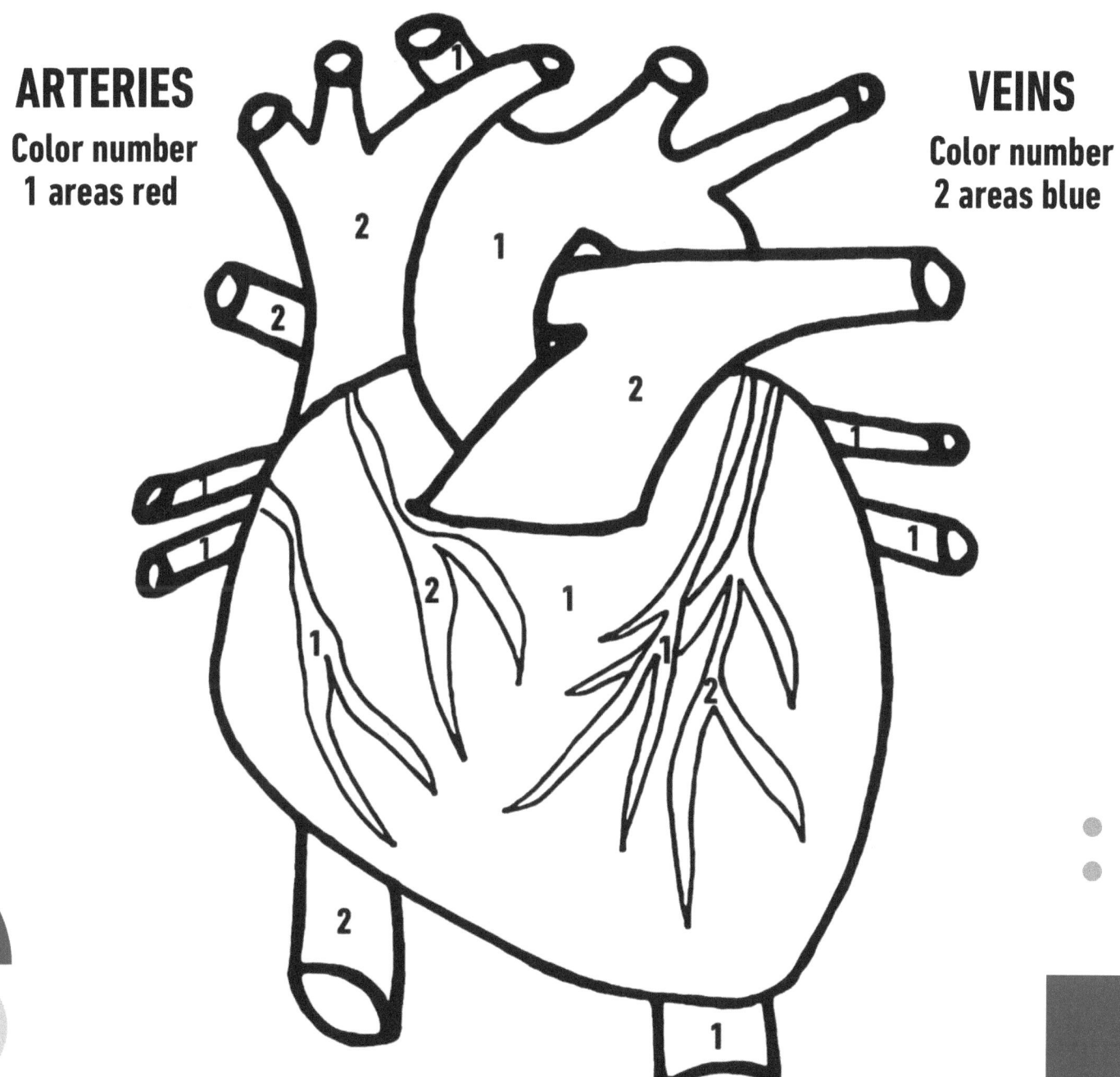

Betcha Didn't Know!

BLACK WOMEN IN HISTORY CRAFT AND ACTIVITY BOOK

Thank you for completing my book! Let me know your favorite activity on my instagram @AmariAri! I can't wait to hear from you!

–Amari 😊

Betcha Didn't Know!

BLACK WOMEN IN HISTORY
CRAFT AND ACTIVITY BOOK

Amari Robinson is a trailblazing 15 year old and oldest daughter of Richard and Mari Robinson. Amari is an amazing student and she loves to play soccer! She has been homeschooled her entire schooling life and through that, she was able to gain a passion and love for coding and is a bonafide software engineer! She has three apps on the Apple App Store that she has built on her own and she has built code that is a part of the mobile app, Grub Trucks.

Amari hosts a weekly podcast called Betcha Didn't Know! that is all about bringing awareness and spreading knowledge of amazing African American women. She built a mobile app and website of the same name as companions to her podcast.

Amari and her little sister own the company, AmariAri where they use their creativity to create apparel and accessories. She loves to help out with her parents' nonprofit, Hack for Community, where she tells of her love for coding to other teens and kids. She is also a junior board member of the nonprofit, Speak Life Now Inc. Amari is the 2022 Miss Teen Junior Miss of New Kent County. She has also the recipient of the Shooting Star Award of the Community Leaders Brunch in 2019, the Youth ImpactING the Community Award in 2022 and the Community Heroes award in 2023. She is also an active member of the Youth Council for New Kent County branch of the NAACP. Amari loves gardening and spending time with her siblings, her parents, and her family.

Check out her products on amariari.com as well as her mobile apps, Betcha Didn't Know!, AmariAri Stickers, and the Betcha Didn't Know Apple Watch App all available on the Apple App Store.

www.ingramcontent.com/pod-product-compliance
Lightning Source LLC
Chambersburg PA
CBHW040054160426
43192CB00002B/68